I love the farm

priddy books
big ideas for little people

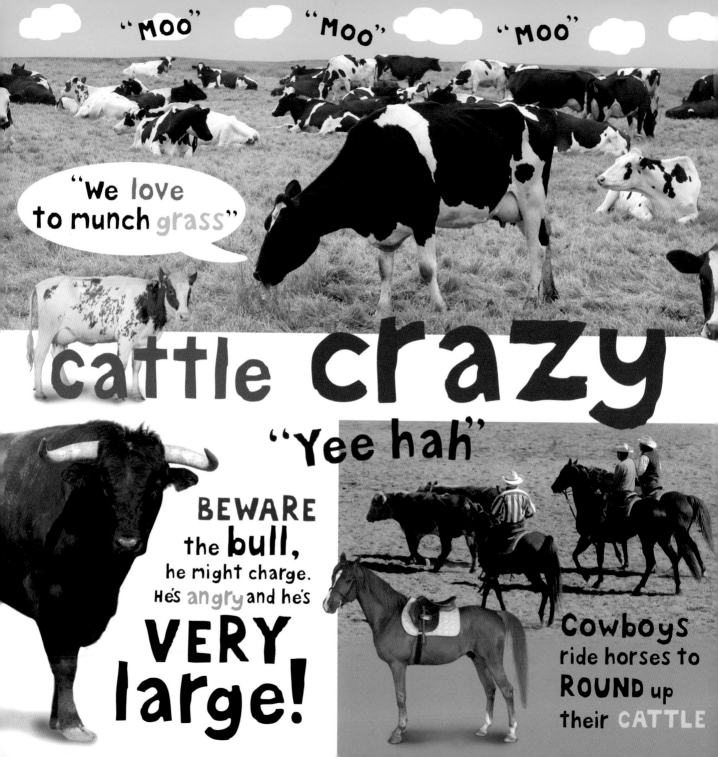

what **FOOD** do we get from cows?

Butter

USE it to cover **TOAST** or bread, it's everybody's FAVORITE spread

milk

DO you like **cold** milk before bed? or perhaps a **HOT** chocolate instead?

WHOLE MILK
HOMOGENIZED • PASTEURIZED

milk

cream IS DELICIOUS poured on **desserts!**

mmm... cheese... **?** HOW MANY different **cheeses** have you tried?

Turkey

The turkey is
a funny bird,
his **gobble**
noise I'm sure
you've **HEARD**

Drake

A **male** duck is called
a DRAKE, he likes to
hang out by the **lake**

Noi
bil

A group of **geese** is called a **GAGGLE**

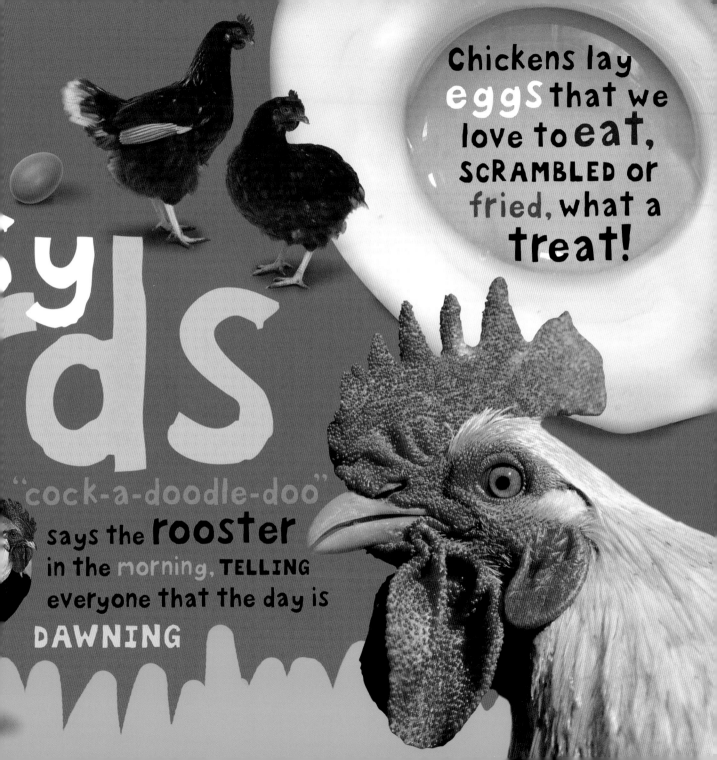

Chickens lay **eggs** that we love to **eat**, SCRAMBLED or fried, what a **treat!**

ʸdS

"cock-a-doodle-doo" says the **rooster** in the morning, TELLING everyone that the day is **DAWNING**

Woolly friends

In SUMMERTIME we **shear** their coats, but it doesn't hurt the sheep or goats

Llamas might look rather SCRUFFY, but their coats are soft and fluffy!

MALE goats are called billy GOATS

"Let's eat those flowers!"

Pink piglets are so very sweet,
they grow because they EAT and EAT

Perfect pigs

Rolling in MUD
is great fun,
it helps pigs cool
off in the
hot sun!

Stable

When it turns COLD LATE in the year, the chilly horse is put in HERE

Horsing around

STANDING UP when **a few hours old,** the newborn **foals** are very BOLD

The **shire horses** are big and strong - they used to PULL the PLOW along

This man's name is **Farmer BOB,** he's always **BUSY** with a **JOB**

The VET VISITS the **farm,** to check the animals **HAVEN'T** come to HARM

Friend

DONKEYS have HUGE ears!

Sheepdog I help the **farmer** round up **Sheep** in the **FIELDS**

"Quack quack" says the duck with her ducklings in line, we must **HURRY** to get to the pond on time

S and **families**

cats
No **farm** is complete without some **CATS**, they **run around** and **catch** the **RATS!**

An ORCHARD is where **apples** are found, some on the **trees** and **SOME** on the ground

DO you LIKE to eat **cereal** for breakfast?

Far foo

Bread
DO yOU have a favorite **SPREAD** to **put** on to your toast or **BREAD?**

carrots
Rabbits love on carrots wit

Eating **LETTUCE** keeps **YOU** healthy!

Red or **yellow**, sour or sweet, **tomatoes** grow best in the **HEAT**

m

ods

which **potato** do you like the most? **MASHED** or baked, boiled or **roast?**

o munch and munch, heir tasty **CRUNCH**

wheat is **GROUND** into **flour** to make **BREAD** and **cakes**

BUNCHES of **grapes** **GROW** on a **VINE**, **THEY're** picked and **SQUASHED** and made into **wine!**

Made from **cocoa** beans, it's **tasty** and **Sweet.** DO you like to EAT chocolate as a **TREAT?**

mmm..... delicious **COFFEE!**

sunflower **SEEDS** can be MADE into oil for COOKING

Busy **bees** make lots of **HONEY**, sticky and sweet, and often RUNNY!

In countries sunny and **HOT**, LOOK out for lemon trees - they're not **HARD** to spot

Tractor
Painted red, blue or GREEN, it's everyone's FAVORITE farm machine

Lifting and SHIFTING seed and grain, **front loader** drives down the lane

Tracked tractor's good when the going's TOUGH, it travels over ground so rough

The **baler** makes bales from hay,
for ANIMALS to eat all day

Busy machines

Telescopic forklift

Lifting UP and DOWN is
this machine's role,
it's a **ZIPPY** truck that's
tricky to **CONTROL**

The PLOW turns over the soil so that seeds can be PLANTED

To **TEAR** around the **farm** at **speed,** a nippy **quad** is what you **NEED**

Taking a **HORSE** to a race or show, the **horsecar** is the way to go

This **trailer** carries **SHEEP** aplenty, they travel in groups of **more than 20!**

Combine harvester At harvest time **it never STOPS,** it's when I must **collect the CROPS!**

CHICKS
"cheep cheep"

MOUSE
"squeak squeak"

DUCK
"quack quack"

Farm
noises

"oink oink"
PIG

"moo moo"
COW

"baa baaa"
SHEEP

"cock-a-doodle-doo"
ROOSTER